THE LEGEND OF MOE NORMAN

The Man With the Perfect Swing

Andrew Podnieks

Library and Archives Canada Cataloguing in Publication

Podnieks, Andrew
The Legend of Moe Norman: The Man With the Perfect Swing

ISBN 978-0-9867964-1-8

Moydart Press
www.andrewpodnieks.com

First Printing 2012

Printed and bound in China

Contents

Introduction

There are two absolutes about golfer Moe Norman. One, he was a bit of an oddball character; two, he was the greatest ball-striker to pass through our universe.

To the former, most people refer to an incident that occurred when Norman was five years old. He and a friend "miraculously escaped injury and possible death," according to a local newspaper report, when they were tobogganing on a small street in Kitchener. They landed underneath a car, and it appeared Murray suffered only a slight bruise to his cheek when they hit it. His mother later admitted, though, that she should have taken him to the hospital for possible head trauma. This is the usual explanation given for Norman's quick speech and repetitive patterns which marked his style of conversation.

But he was peculiar in other ways as well. He was shy to the point of being reclusive, never lived in a formal apartment he could call home, never drank alcohol, never married, maintained a poor diet, and spent just about every minute of every day consumed by golf.

As to his swing, Norman came by that honestly, boasting that anyone could hit the ball as well as he—all they had to do was hit 600 balls a day every day for five or six years. Although Norman's swing was, in fact, awkward-looking if not downright ugly, the flight of his ball was a majestic work of art, a thing of gravitational beauty that no golfer could match. Not Nicklaus, not Palmer, not Tiger, not Ernie.

Murray Herbert Norman was born in Kitchener, Ontario, on July 10, 1929, with twin sister, Marie. They were two of six children, but only Murray was inclined to sports as a kid. He didn't like school and went to the golf course so often he was finally expelled from classes. "I was never there," Norman admitted.

Not surprisingly, the one subject he loved and excelled at was math. He was nothing short of brilliant with numbers and later in life was famous for being able to rhyme off the yardage and scores of every hole on most of the golf courses he played, even decades after his last round.

Norman started as a caddy at Rockway Golf Course in Kitchener and soon after frequented the more prestigious Westmount Golf & Country Club. He used his pay to buy his first set of clubs ten cents at a time. He wasn't that good, but he was determined, and through trial and error on his own he figured out a style of holding the club and addressing the ball that was unique, eccentric, thoroughly unconventional—and brilliantly effective.

During his teen years friends and patrons around the club never called him Murray. Instead, he was nicknamed "Moe the Schmoe." That was soon shortened to Moe, the name he used the rest of his life.

But as much as his swing made him famous, there were other elements to his style that were the stuff of legend. Just as he spoke quickly, he played quickly. Nothing threw him off his game more than slow play, and slow play for Norman was defined as anything short of lightning fast play. He never lined up a shot, and oftentimes he teed off by tossing a ball to the ground and hitting it without the benefit of a tee. Upon striking the ball, he was off down the fairway, and he played his next shot just as quickly as his last.

On the green, Norman never lined up a putt. He walked up to the ball, steadied himself, and stroked the ball. This was where he was subject to criticism, though, because putting is such a crucial element to scoring well. He hated practising putting—it was a stroke that wasn't a "swing" stroke—and it was always the part of the game that did him in at critical moments. Norman boasted that a good game of golf should come in under two hours, and when he got to serious competition and opponents took their time to prepare for a shot, he became noticeably agitated and his own play suffered.

Norman won many a small and local tournament during his early years, but he came to national prominence in the mid-1950s by winning the Canadian Amateur championship in '55 and '56. His victories, however, were in some ways overshadowed by his seeming disregard for his amateur status. Never wealthy, he often sold his prizes for cash—sometimes before the tournament began!—because he needed the money and he didn't need yet another television, toaster, or watch. But, as the RCGA pointed out, profiting from golf was against rules of amateur play.

These national wins, though, caught the attention of the executives of the Masters in Augusta, Georgia, and twice Norman was invited to play. The first time, 1956, he had to withdraw because of hands so badly blistered from practise that he couldn't hold the club. The second time, he missed the cut. In both years he was as perfect as expected from tee to green, but he didn't have the patience to master the fast and undulating greens of the Augusta National Golf Club.

In 1959, Norman turned pro, believing he could now finance his career and win enough money to earn a modest living. The dream of playing on the PGA Tour, though, was short-lived. Norman played just six events in his first year and five the next. His best result was a fourth place finish at the Greater New Orleans Open in March 1959. Consensus had it that the shy and sensitive Norman could not endure the many jibes about his comportment that he was subject to by colleagues on the tour and fans around the U.S.. He wore turtlenecks in the heat of summer. His teeth were bad from too many Cokes and not enough dental care. The six-inch tees which were a hoot for the fans at small tournaments in Canada were out of favour with the serious golfers. He looked funny, walked funny, talked funny, and swung funny. Norman returned to Canada and, with few exceptions, never played professionally in the U.S. again.

By now, though, Norman's reputation was firmly entrenched in the mind of the golfing world, and he was more comfortable with his lofty place in that world. Perhaps he wasn't cut out for top tournament play, but his swing was the envy of every serious golfer on the planet. Norman was happy to teach and give clinics, and he loved the attention of the top PGA golfers when they asked him to hit some balls. But he was denied the one thing he craved more than any other—respect from the Royal Canadian Golf Association.

In the end, the RCGA inducted him into Canada's golf hall of fame in 1995 when he was 65. The RCGA was more or less shamed into honouring Moe simply because his reputation had perhaps exceeded the reputation of the RCGA itself. No, Moe didn't win several PGA Tour events like George Knudson, and he wasn't the pretty boy who appeared in golf magazines for his style and drama, but he hit the ball straighter more consistently than any golfer in the history of the game. Norman was inducted because of his swing, and that's the essence of any golfer's game.

At the time of his death on September 4, 2004, Norman's car resembled an apartment more than a vehicle. It had ten pairs of golf shoes, hundreds of balls and thousands of tees, a plethora of clubs, clothes, books, notepads, and some $20,000 in cash. He didn't trust many people and didn't let many people into his personal life, but his golfing life—his stroke—defined his existence, and that, more than anything, is what people will always remember about him. Moe Norman—the man with the perfect swing.

ANDREW PODNIEKS

Two legends met at the practise green one day when Tiger Woods and
Moe Norman shook hands.

The Swing

Swinging a golf club and making proper contact with a ball is a feat that consists of dozens of small movements in quick succession. Obviously it's not easy or more people would be better at it, but Moe Norman was famous not only for the effectiveness of his swing but also its unorthodox appearance and its economy. Perhaps what is most amazing of all is that his swing resembled nothing and borrowed no element from any other golfer. In truth, he more or less created a swing out of the ether.

For starters, Moe's body position was awkward looking. He spread his feet wide apart and had no bend to his knees. From his hips to feet was one rigid zone. His arms were also rigid and outstretched, as though they were trying desperately to reach the ball while being restricted by feet planted too far away. Moe's arm position created one line from his chest to the ball, single plane, if you will, to create a uniform swing that, as many people observed, most resembled a ball-hitting machine.

During Moe's swing, the club moved in a perfect plane with his body. His wrists were firm and powerful. They hinged perfectly to place the club at the perfect angle at the top the golf swing. In Moe's best playing years, he used the Vardon grip, eventually changing to a ten-finger grip in his later years. But Moe's hands were so well positioned on the club, the slight difference between grips didn't matter. It was the perfect position of the hands that mattered.

The top of his top (left) hand faced the target, which is common, but his lower was rotated more under the shaft so the club aligned with his right arm, perfecting his unique single plane. This meant a firmer grip, less likelihood of movement of the club in the hand, and a more consistent stroke upon impact each time. As well, Norman used very thick grips on his clubs making it easier to hold them firmly. He often called other players' clubs "matchsticks" because they had narrow grips.

As well, golfers typically hold the club like a bouquet of flowers—gently. Moe gripped it like a vice, trying to squeeze the club into dust. The result was a club with little movement or waggle, little to throw it off line or alter its course through impact.

With an almost perfectly rigid body, there were fewer body parts moving around during the backswing, impact, and follow through. Norman did what every golfer hopes to do but can never quite figure out—how to simplify the swing and reduce the number of movements needed to hit the ball.

Norman's setup also helped facilitate what he thought was the most important part of the swing—maintaining the clubface square to the target for as long as possible. Norman created an exercise he practised for thousands of hours. He put a coin 41 inches behind the ball and another one 22 inches ahead of the ball. These points, with the tee, formed a perfectly straight line. He then made sure his clubface started on the back coin and clipped the front coin after impact with the ball to ensure the clubface was as square to the target as possible. To accentuate this, he finished his swing by following through in an upward motion, not a sideways motion as is most common.

The other Normanesque characteristic one might notice is that all of these elements combined ensured that he had one fluid swing from start to finish. All other golfers take the club back one way, but as they transfer their weight from back to front then change the path of the club on the downswing. As a result, making error on contact between the clubface and ball becomes far more likely.

Norman had his irons built radically differently from most every other golfer. He made sure the lie of each club in his bag was the same, from 2-iron down to pitching wedge. What this meant was that the angle of every club (between the clubface and the shaft) was the same, so he was the same distance to the ball regardless what club he used. Most golfers stand closer to the ball the lower the club (i.e., the greater the loft) because of a greater lie.

Moe's swing relied heavily on his shoulders for power and on his hips for balance and stability, something no other golfer does to the same extent. That is, as he went through his backswing and then transferred weight and power from back to front, his hips moved only a little bit. But his shoulders twisted 90 degrees or more. This meant that his body was rock solid, but his arms were full of strength as they whipped through the downswing and made contact with the ball.

At the same time, his wide stance anchored his legs to the ground so he couldn't overhit or pull his clubface out of alignment. "I let my swing balance me," is how Moe described it. Just as his set position was a straight line from his shoulders through the arms, hands, and blade of the club, so, too, was his finish perfectly straight. You could draw a line from his right foot through his body, arms, and club which was now high in the sky, a perfectly straight finish on follow through.

But perhaps the most telling fact of Moe's swing was the trajectory of the ball. Anyone who watches golf on television sees that most shots have spin on them. The ball lands on the green and then rolls back because of spin. But every ball also rolls a little left or right because the flight of the ball is never straight. When Titleist studied Moe's swing, however, researchers discovered Moe had virtually no side spin, meaning his ball was 99.9 per cent straight. Every time.

Two other things about Moe's swing. Just to look at him anyone could see he was neither big nor particularly athletic, yet his swing was so perfect that he was one of the longest hitters around. As well, he hit the ball as straight and as long later in life as anyone else did who was decades younger. Said Mike Weir: "To watch Moe, in his seventies, hit the ball better than most of us guys [PGA Tour pros] on the range was pretty neat to see."

Moe addresses the ball in a unique manner. Standing far away from the ball with arms firm and outstretched, he keeps his swing in one line (one plane) to reduce the number of moving parts and keep the swing consistent from start to finish.

Moe keeps the clubface on the target longer than any golfer, and he follows through high and straight rather than back and to the side, ensuring a straighter shot all the time.

The Stories

Moe's presence was always most noteworthy at the Canadian Open when the world's top pros gathered once a year. The greatest players often asked Moe for a demonstration of his swing, and he always obliged, honoured to be among the world's best golfers. Ben Crenshaw was among that group one year and marveled at Moe's abilities. "People who've never seen him wouldn't know from someone's description how good he is. You have to see it to believe it. He's slightly unorthodox, but the only thing you have to see is the ball going to the target—every time."

Played at the Scarboro Golf and Country Club in the east end of Toronto, the 1955 Labatt Open turned out to be critical to Moe's career. "I finished as low amateur," he explained. "I always tried to give the people a show, teeing my ball on Coca-Cola bottles, that sort of thing. When the tournament was over, Conn Smythe, the famous owner of the Toronto Maple Leafs, approached me. "What are you doing this winter?" he asked. "Going back to setting my pins [at the bowling alley]," I said. "Well, I like a guy who has colour," Mr. Smythe said. "You're too good to be setting pins." Mr. Smythe gave me $5,000 and sent me to Florida. He let me stay in his place at The Breakers." The monetary gift violated golf's rules for amateurs, but neither man cared. "I wouldn't have kept playing [in the winter] if it wasn't for him," Moe acknowledged of Smythe's munificence. "He kept my future in golf going. Nobody in Kitchener would help me."

Wayne Gretzky once played a round of golf with Moe at the Brantford Golf & Country Club. "Afterwards," Norman related, "he told me I was one of the smartest athletes he had ever met, that he would like to be around me more."

"It's amazing, the money these guys make playing the PGA Tour. It's good for them but bad for the fans because the players don't need to play very often. They've got a lot, and they know most of the rest is going to the government anyway, so what's the use?"
—Moe Norman

Moe once hit 146 drives on the practice range without having to touch his tee, so clean was his striking of the ball.

Moe had another hockey connection in the form of Bill Mitchell. Mitchell was a "one-game wonder" in the NHL, playing a single game for Detroit in 1963-64 during a 20-year pro career. He also happened to be an excellent golfer and served as assistant pro to Lloyd Tucker at the Rockway Golf Club in Kitchener. Bill's son, Lawson, closer to Moe's age, became a friend of Moe and saw Moe develop during his early and formative years.

"Sometimes you need 10 more yards out of a drive. There's only one proper way to do that, and it's turning your shoulders more. It's the only way to keep your rhythm. Every other method—swinging faster or with more effort, changing your ball position or anything else—will cost you accuracy. It has to. Otherwise, you'd swing that way every time."
—Moe Norman

"Working on your swing is the greatest joy in golf. Tiger Woods must be having a wonderful time searching for that one little thing he's doing wrong. I wonder when he'll notice it—the way his right heel lifts straight off the ground now instead of coming up and toward his left. His weight shift is terrible right now, that's all. Don't tell him. It'll ruin his fun."
—Moe Norman

Moe and his friends often played at
a course called Golf Haven in Ontario.
On one hole, after hitting their drives,
Moe vanished into the forest, retuning
a few minutes later. Moe was teased
for having to deal with Mother Nature
at an inopportune time, but he corrected
his pals. "I had to grab some money,"
he explained, showing off a wad of
bills that counted into the thousands
of dollars. Moe had buried it in the
forest months earlier, returning
to collect it when he needed it.

"I had a chance to play with [Moe] on many occasions. He was really enjoyable to play with. He was a phenom. I tell people stories about how good he was, but they don't believe me. He'd tell me and show me things about the swing, but of course he had such an unorthodox style, different than anybody else, with a big grip way out from his body and a wide stance. So I never tried to play that way. But he was so much fun to play with."

—Wayne Gretzky

> "I hit with effortless power.
> Everyone else hits with
> powerless effort."
> —Moe Norman

An undated story from the 1950s.
Moe and Ben Hogan were hitting
practice shots beside each other.
Hogan assertively said there was
no such thing as a straight golf shot.
Moe raised an eyebrow mischievously
and proceeded to hit one ball after
another after another dead straight.
Hogan walked away telling Moe to,
"keep hitting those accidents."

In his youth, Moe's greatest weakness on the course was hooking the ball. He believed this was because the club-face was not flush on point of contact and figured the remedy was simple—clutch the club with all his strength so it wouldn't wiggle during his swing. So, his grip resembled holding a baseball bat more than a golf club. He cut many strokes off his score, but his hands blistered badly, got calloused, and often bled after hitting several hundred golf balls a day. Sometimes the callouses were so thick he had to scrape them off with a razor blade or scissors.

"I never got married. In fact, I went on only three dates. If I'd gotten married, it wouldn't have been fair to a wife because of my life as a golfer. I'd wind up divorced, and then she'd get everything. I think that's how it works, judging by what's happened to some friends of mine. I'm very happy being alone."
—Moe Norman

"I'd sleep in bunkers," Moe confessed of his early days going to tournaments. "Twice I woke up, snakes across my legs. In bunkers! That's all I could afford. I only had enough money for the entry fee, but I loved it. What else could I do? I loved the game so much, and I wanted to be good. This is what I had to do, or I couldn't go to the tournaments."

One time a young Moe was caddying for the much older and, at the time, more accomplished Nick Weslock at a tournament. Standing on the tee of a par three, Weslock asked his caddy for a seven iron. Moe refused to hand over the club, saying the hole required no more than an eight iron. When Weslock questioned Moe, Moe said that if Weslock hit the seven he'd walk away and force Weslock to carry his own clubs for the rest of the day. Weslock hit the eight iron to within three feet of the pin, birdied the hole, and won the tournament.

Moe's first appearance at the Masters in Augusta, Georgia, in 1956 was noteworthy in many ways. First, in typical Moe fashion, he teed off even while his name was still being announced. He then started down the fairway carrying his own bag, shocking the venerable club's directors who instantly provided him with a caddy. ("They paid for him, too," Moe boasted.) Despite horrible putting (six three putts), he carded a 75, but while practising later in the day he was approached by the great Sam Snead. "He gave me a 40-minute lesson," Moe explained, "telling me to hit my irons like a fairway wood, meaning to sweep it instead of hitting down on it.

I was in awe, and like a dumbbell I proceeded to hit 800 balls." The result was bloody and badly damaged hands. Moe was forced to withdraw midway through the third round, the pain too great to endure. "My right thumb swelled up so big I couldn't hit a ball without terrible pain. That was the last lesson I took, let me tell you."

Moe had to change his personality
a little bit when he turned pro.
No more driving off Coke bottles
or six-inch tees, and no more crowd-
pleasing shenanigans. "I don't putt
one-handed through my legs
anymore," he said, downcast.

Moe was always happier entertaining
on the course than taking the game too
seriously. On one Canadian Tour event
he held a three-shot lead standing on
the final hole. He reached the par five
in two, then putted his third shot into
a nearby bunker before getting up
and down for par and the victory.
The crowd showered him with laughter
and applause in equal measure.

"Your mind is the generator, your body is the motor. The club is the trigger, and the ball is a bullet. Take aim and fire!"—Moe Norman

"Going through the ball, I feel my right hand is a claw. No hinging of my right wrist at all. I just gather the ball up. No supination or pronation. On the follow-through I shake hands with the flagstick."
—Moe Norman

One early morning Moe was out with friend Ken Venning, playing Tomoka Oaks Golf Course in Daytona Beach, Florida. At the 10th tee, Moe hit three drives, and when they got to the balls in the fairway Tomoka saw all three were touching. "You could see the lines in the dew where they rolled up against each other," Tomoka recalled incredulously.

"Even in my late teens and early twenties, when I got good enough to play in tournaments, I slept in bunkers and hitchhiked to get from one place to the next. Some of the golfers laughed like hell at me and teased me constantly—"Where you sleeping tonight, Moe?" Nobody came to my rescue until I was 26. I really resented that."

—Moe Norman

"With a titanium driver I'm hitting it farther now than when I was 35, and that's the truth. It doesn't satisfy me; it bothers me. Do I want to hit the ball farther when I'm 100 than I do now? No. It wouldn't be right. All anyone cares about is hitting it farther—even with the irons. Hitting the ball pure and accurate is more rewarding than hitting it far. Don't forget that, ever."
—Moe Norman

One story that speaks to Moe's
reputation but has never been
verified tells of Moe using three
matches to set up a tee-pee
for a tee and then hitting the
ball so perfectly off it that
the matches ignited as
the ball took flight!

"There's only one secret in the game, and that's hard work."
—Moe Norman

In 1956, the RCGA took Moe off Canada's entry for the America's Cup because he had violated amateur laws by repeatedly earning money from golf. Some income came in the form of clinics, some from selling his prizes from tournaments, but as Moe asked rhetorically, "What am I supposed to do with 27 watches?" The decision eventually forced Moe to turn pro, in January 1959, with the announcement that he had found, "the means of paying my expenses in order to play competitive golf."

Moe's second, and last, appearance at the Master's was as disappointing as his first. For starters, 1957 marked the first time the tournament had a cut line. That is, after two rounds the top players continued playing while players with lower scores were sent home. Second, Moe continued to be bedeviled by the greens despite perfect play from tee to green. He shot a 77-74 and missed the cut, went home, and never played the event again. Moe's partner for the two rounds was Bob Rothberg who said Moe hit 18 of 18 fairways in regulation and 17 of 18 greens. Putting was his downfall.

"Backing the ball up on the green may look impressive, but it's no way to play golf, because you can't control it. Every shot you hit should bounce forward after it lands. If the flagstick is just over a bunker, you get it close by hitting the ball higher, not by backing it up. With these 60-degree wedges, hitting it high is easy."

—Moe Norman

Moe's philosophy: "I live one day at a time. I always believe this is my last day, not that tomorrow is my first day. Live the best you can—that's my idea. I still hit hundreds of balls a day. That's what I do. I believe what Hogan said at the '56 Masters on the putting green. Every day you don't hit balls is one day longer it takes you to get better."

"I swing through the ball, not at it."
—Moe Norman

Lee Trevino, again on Moe's abilities. "I do not know of any player who could strike a golf ball like Moe Norman as far as hitting it solid, knowing where it's going, knowing the mechanics of the game, and knowing what he wanted to do with the golf ball. When you're talking about Moe Norman, you're talking about a legend, and I'm talking about a living legend because the public doesn't know Moe Norman. Ask any golf professional, whether you're in Australia, the U.S., or Great Britain, and they say that it's the Canadian guy who hits it so damn good. I'd say, 'yes, that's him.' He's a legend with the professionals. The guy's a genius."

"Only two players have ever truly owned their swings—Moe Norman and Ben Hogan," Tiger Woods said. "I want to own mine. That's where the satisfaction comes from."

In the winter, Moe used to work for a bowling alley, setting up the pins. The alley also happened to be near an indoor golf school where Moe would go every day to hit balls when the weather was inclement. "In the 1950s," Moe explained, "there was no money to be made playing professionally in Canada. I stayed an amateur, working as a pin-setter in a bowling alley all winter so I could play golf all summer. This was before they had machines that set the pins. That was hard work, but, boy, was I good at it. I was able to work four lanes at once because they played with five pins, not ten. I hopped from one lane to the next like a bumblebee. No one was faster or better than me."

"If I hit a bad shot, I just laughed. It's part of the game. It's a walk in the park, a walk in the park."
—Moe Norman

Moe made history on July 16, 1957, at Rockway, the course he knew and loved so well. Playing with Gary Cowan in a foursome, Moe played a flawless round of golf. He capped the day with a birdie putt from six feet at the 18th hole. That gave him a 59 and a place in golf history. His card was bronzed by the club and can be seen there still. "It could have been lower if I hadn't three-putted the 10th hole," Moe said of his great day. "In fact, I didn't putt all that well that day. I hit the ball close a lot, is all."

George Knudson was in line at a casual restaurant when he told a friend that Moe Norman was the best ball striker in the world. Knudson hadn't known that Moe was right behind him. Moe started to cry, so moved was he by the great compliment from a world-class golfer. "Moe is the most sensitive man I know," Knudson said.

"I don't believe in taking much of a divot, especially with the longer irons. You want to barely comb the grass through impact, as though you were hitting a ball off the top of somebody's crew cut. It's the only way to catch the ball on the second groove up from the bottom of the clubface. That's where you want to make contact—on the second groove."

—Moe Norman

In 1969, Moe played an exhibition in Toronto with Sam Snead and Ed Oliver. When the threesome got to the 16th tee, they saw a hole with a creek running through the fairway about 250 yards ahead. Snead decided the wise play was to lay up in front of the water and hit his approach to the green from the near side. He then suggested Moe do the same. Norman, however, pulled out a driver from his bag. "I'm not aiming to clear the water," Moe explained. "I'm aiming for the bridge." Confused, Snead watched as Moe's drive hit the bridge and bounced far over the water. Snead was silent for the rest of the game.

Moe boasted that over the course of one eleven-year period of his career, nearly a quarter of a million golf shots, he hit only one out of bounds—and that by just a couple of feet.

"You are what you think you are."
—Moe Norman

Always impatient when not actually striking the ball, Moe had a habit of bouncing a ball off the face of a club while walking down the fairway or to a green. One fan wagered Moe that he couldn't bounce a ball 100 times in a row. For every one less than 100, Moe had to pay the fan one dollar, and for every bounce over one hundred, the fan had to pay Moe a dollar. Moe intentionally missed at 184, feeling the fan had suffered due humiliation by losing $84. "It was enough," Moe said. "Anyway, the guy's jaw was dropping a little lower every time."

Norman's reputation as "the clown prince of golf" gained momentum later in 1948 after his first win. On his way to a tournament in Hamilton with three other golfers from Rockway, their home course, their car broke down. A local mechanic offered the boys a lift in his dump truck, which pulled up to the first tee creating a thick cloud of dust just as Moe's name was being announced at the first tee. Moe literally ran from the truck, pulling a club from his bag at the same time, teed up a ball, and smacked it down the centre of the fairway in one seemingly continuous motion. "I changed into my golf shoes while walking down the first fairway," he added.

"He [Moe Norman] woke up every morning knowing he would hit it well. He just knew he was going to hit it well. Every day. It's frightening how straight he hit it."
—Tiger Woods

Golfing with NHL legend Stan Mikita in St. Catharines one day, Moe asked Stan for advice as they stood in the tee box at the 9th hole. Mikita said the hole called for an easy driver and wedge. Moe took out his wedge and hit, played a driver from the middle of the fairway, and reached the green in two, just as he had been advised.

Ken Venturi, who gave Moe the nickname "Pipeline," admired Moe's range of skills in figuring out what kind of a shot to hit. "Moe had more varied shots than anyone I'd ever seen...I could never do some of the shots he could...like hitting a driver out of a divot."

In December 1997, Moe was taken
to hospital by ambulance after a heart
attack scare. He was transported by
ambulance from Kitchener to the
London Health Sciences Centre, and
at one point things didn't look so good
for Norman. A nurse asked Moe if he
knew where he was, and Moe quickly
said, "Sure—the third hole." Worried,
hospital staff continued to question
him until one senior member realized the
hospital was situated on what used to be
the third hole of the London Hunt Club,
a course Norman played some four
decades earlier. Not only that, Moe
proceeded to reel off the yardage of each
hole and how to navigate the course,
all of which checked out when
someone went to the trouble of
finding an old scorecard.

In 1958, Moe decided to buy a car so that he could spend the winter in Florida golfing. He asked a friend to help him find one with a big trunk and ended up buying a Cadillac. Moe paid $2,600 for the car—in cash, with 26 crisp hundred-dollar bills. This was Moe's *modus operandi*. He bought a new used car every year, always paying cash. Moe distrusted banks and hid money in every conceivable nook and cranny of his car instead. When he died, there was some $20,000 stashed in his Cadillac.

"**If you fear failure,
you lose before you start.**"
—Moe Norman

Moe had only one coach, Lloyd Tucker,
and that when Moe was just starting
to play. Tucker described Moe like this:
"If you've seen Astaire, you've seen
the best dancer. If you've seen Peggy
Fleming, you've seen the best skater.
And if you see Moe hit a golf ball,
you know you've seen the best
to ever hit a golf ball."

An Australian golfer asked Moe to hit some shots so the visitor could watch the master's swing. Norman borrowed the Aussie's driver and hit about 30 balls without the tee so much a moving a millimetre. "I can't believe you can do that," the awestruck Australian said. "Didn't come here to hit tees. Didn't come here to hit tees. Came here to hit the ball," Moe replied.

"I hit so many balls I wore out three sets of irons. I'd wear the grooves down to nothing and then go even farther, so there was a concave area the size of a dime on the sweet spot. Eventually the ball would start to fly a little crooked from catching the sides of that pockmark, and the clubs became illegal because the faces weren't flat."

—Moe Norman

The RCGA got so frustrated by Moe's quick play that it took unusual measures to ensure patrons could adequately get into position for tee shots and follow play. This happened at the 1956 Canadian Amateur Open in Edmundston, New Brunswick, while Norman was playing alongside the equally fast Jerry Magee. "Magee and I played the first nine holes in 58 minutes," Moe boasted with a pride that was not enjoyed equally by tournament officials. "The RCGA held us back on the final nine," Moe continued. "They had a Jeep parked in front of all the tees, so we couldn't hit our tee shots until the crowd caught up."

The first time Moe discovered his passion for golf came in the simplest way. He and brother Ron would use braches to hit a ball aimed at a small hole they dug at each end of the neighbourhood playground. A little later in childhood, using real clubs and balls, he'd hit literally around houses and streets, breaking windows left, right, and centre, much to the anger of his father who usually had to pay for the damages.

> # "Stop worrying about when you're going to die but how you will live."
> ## —Moe Norman

Ernie Hauser was another childhood friend and golf partner with Moe at Rockway. Hauser once recalled the economy of Moe's bag. "You'd see him in the parking lot at Rockway before a game pulling clubs out of his bag." Moe would say, "The wind is blowing down number 6, so I don't need my five-iron, and it's blowing up 10, so I don't need my four-iron." Hauser was amazed. "He knew the clubs he'd hit on every hole, so it wouldn't weight the bag down. I thought, 'no one's that good!'"

Moe in an undated school photo (seated front row, far left).

Moe holds court for some of the world's best players, notably Nick Faldo, Ben Crenshaw, Fred Couples, and Nick Price.

Moe's backswing is compact and strong while his legs stay wide apart for balance.

Only after he follows through does he lift his right foot.

Moe follows through the ball while keeping his clubface directed at the target for as long as possible.

Moe has an unusually high finish to maintain consistent ball flight.

STROKES	PAR	YARDS	MOE NORMAN	BOB PATTERSON	WON.	HOLE.	LOST	LLOYD NIZIOL	GARY COWAN	C. CLGH
8	4	369	4	4		1		4	3	4
12	4	324	4	4		2		5	4	4
10	3	165	(2)	8		3		3	3	3
4	4	425	4	5		4		4	5	5
17	3	162	3	3		5		3	3	3
7	4	395	4	6		6		6	4	4
1	5	508	(3)	5		7		5	4	5
13	4	315	(3)	4		8		4	4	4
15	4	309	(3)	4		9		4	4	4
	35	2972	30	43		OUT.		38	34	36
6	4	420	5	4		10		5	4	5
11	4	300	3	3		11		4	4	4
14	3	168	3	4		12		3	3	3
5	4	425	4	5		13		5	4	5
16	3	203	(2)	3		14		3	3	3
2	5	500	(3)	5		15		5	4	5
18	3	145	(2)	3		16		3	3	3
3	5	464	(4)	5		17		5	4	5
9	4	365	(3)	5		18.		4	4	4
IN	35	2990	29	37		IN		37	33	27
OUT	35	2972	30	43		GROSS		38	34	36
TOTAL	70	5962	(59)	80		HNDCP.		75	67	73
						NET.				

REPLACE TURF.

REPLACE TURF.

SIGNED, "Wm. Brimloh" HOSTED. Os Franklin DATE July 16/57

ROCKWAY GOLF CLUB
OPPONENT.

STYMIE GAUGE.

Cecil Manarelle
/OPPONENT.

The scorecard from Moe's masterful round of 59 at Rockway with, among others,
friend Gary Cowan.

(left) A pensive Norman surveys the landscape.

(below) Moe enjoys a soft drink while admiring a photo of him shaking hands with Tiger Woods.

A relaxed Norman hits balls at the practise range.

Even when hitting casually Norman follows through high and at the target.

(above) A lithograph of Moe that hangs in the Moe Norman Museum, in Kitchener.

(left) Later in life Moe promoted Natural Golf which celebrated his swing.

The clean line from Moe's shoulders to the clubface tells the story.

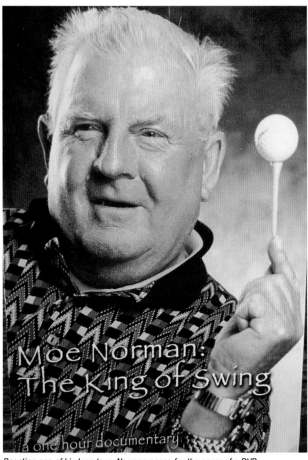

Boasting one of his long tees, Norman poses for the cover of a DVD documentary on his life.

Paul Azinger described Moe's trademark consistency after watching another Moe demonstration of ball striking. "He started ripping these drives right off the ground at the 250-yard marker. He never hit one more than ten yards to either side of it, and he hit at least 50. It was an incredible sight. When he hit irons, he was calling how many times you'd see it bounce after he hit it—sometimes before he hit it—and he'd do it. It was unbelievable."

"In Canada, they like to keep people down. It's true. They can't stand seeing someone become successful, especially if they once were ahead of you. It eats at them, galls them more than they can stand. Canadians go out of their minds with jealousy and will do everything they can to drag you down."
—Moe Norman

Two saviours in Moe's
life were Orm and
Verna Membery who
owned a small club
called Golf Haven,
north of Toronto. They
hired him as the golf
pro for the 6,400-yard
layout, allowing him
to enter tournaments
representing Golf Haven
and not having to run
clinics and teach as
much as he would
otherwise had to
have done.

Rockway was where it was at for golf in the early 1950s. It boasted Norman, Gerry Kesselring, and Tony Matlock, three of the finest young golfers in the country. They were nicknamed the "Three Musketeers" as they travelled to tournaments representing Rockway.

"If you get nervous or afraid in tournaments or playing in front of other people, it's because you place too much value on it. You think the competition is more important than it really is. If you stand on the tee and feel like you're about to cross Niagara Falls on a high wire with no safety net, there's no way you'll have enough trust in yourself to pull it off. They say the only way to master that is through experience, and it's true, but all that means is getting to know yourself better. The better you get to know yourself, the more you'll like and trust that person inside. I won a lot of tournaments because I get along with myself really well."

—Moe Norman

"I don't go to church, but I certainly pray a lot. Always have. One of my sisters was a nun, and when I was young my parents dragged me to church by the seat of my pants. God is real—He has to be, because no man could develop the talent I have on his own. I am the world's best ball-striker and teacher because it was His will. Why did He choose me to be the best who ever lived? I don't have the faintest idea. That's why there's a hereafter—so one day I can find out."
—Moe Norman

"Winners see what they want. Losers see what they don't want."
—Moe Norman

"I hated putting, and so did George Knudson, another really good ball-striker on tour. We played against each other in many betting games where putting didn't count. If you missed a fairway, you owed the other guy $20. If you missed a green, you owed $20. If you hit the flagstick, you won $100. When we got to the green we just picked up our balls and went to the next hole. George was very good, but I got the best of him. My best day, I hit the flagstick six times."
—Moe Norman

"I don't like these super-long par 3s where average golfers need a wood to reach them. They're terrible—you hit 15 or more wood shots on the other holes already; that's enough. On the other hand, I don't like par 4s where guys hit irons off the tee. What are these architects thinking about? They're designing courses upside down. They think they're smart, but they're just the opposite."
—Moe Norman

"When money was dear, I'd play with the same ball until it wore out. A balata-covered wound ball had exactly five rounds in it before it got knocked out of round or got too soft. Then it was time to search the bushes for lost balls and root out a new one."
—Moe Norman

"Don't hold the club lightly. That's a mistake because you'll get too wristy. Hold it firmly. You won't hit the ball quite as far, but you'll hit it straighter, which is what this game is about.

If I had a bunch of juniors, I'd teach them to play from the green backward. Short shots first, with emphasis on how to meet the ball solidly. I'd make them touch the green, then walk backward to the tee and touch the tee, and explain why holes are designed the way they are.

Then I'd teach them why everything works—why a putter has so little loft, why the sand wedge is thicker on the bottom than a pitching wedge, and why woods are larger than irons. Those things mean something. Then I'd help them feel the game. Whisper when they hit a ball solid, "Did you feel that? That's what you want." After a time—there's no hurry—I'd finally help them learn the game. That's the technical part. That comes last."

—Moe Norman

The great South African golfer
Gary Player watched Moe swing
and deduced the secret was that
Moe had fewer moving parts to
his swing than anyone else.

> **"I want both feet on the ground when I hit the ball. I want my swing to balance me."**
> **—Moe Norman**

"I was in the clubhouse at Rockway Golf Course, and I overheard a kid telling another kid that he'd left his wedge at another course and that no one had turned it in. I went to my car and got him one, and he was so happy he jumped all over me. I do this often, especially with kids you can tell are a bit poor and don't get these things from their parents. Very often they start crying, they're so happy."
—Moe Norman

"I never saw a doctor until I was 68. It's because I never felt sick. Never had a headache, earache or toothache, and never had a cold. Then one day I had a heart attack. Now I see the doctor every day. All he did was make me give up all the foods I like, meaning liver and onions, hamburgers, hot dogs, chocolate, barbecue potato chips, all that stuff. He made me switch from regular Coke—I drank 15 cans a day on average—to caffeine-free Diet Coke. I've lost 45 pounds, gone from a 42-inch waist to 37. But I sure miss that food."

—Moe Norman

"I'm the best ball striker, by far," Moe once said. "No one else is close. No wasted motion. That's why I'm the best ball striker there is. I see only one thing after each shot. Happiness."

"Don't change your game for one course. If you visit a course with lots of elevated greens and you tend to hit the ball low, don't make a radical change trying to hit the ball high. It'll wreck your game for a week, at least. Play the game you have, accept whatever score you shoot, and move on. There are lots of courses out there, and the one with too many elevated greens isn't a good one. Don't let it goad you into changing."

—Moe Norman

One of the more subtle idiosyncrasies about Moe was that he didn't wear a glove. Virtually every golfer will wear one on the top hand for all shots except around and on the green.

Moe's friend, Ken Venning, related this story about Moe's reputation from the 1971 World Cup at the PGA National Golf Club in Palm Beach Gardens, Florida. The Americans won the event represented by none other than Jack Nicklaus and Lee Trevino. Gary Player was watching Moe on the practice range and started a conversation. "Soon," Venning explained, "Nicklaus wandered over, and then Trevino. They were watching Moe hit balls and asking him how he hit the ball to peak so that it fell straight down. He [Moe] didn't feel threatened at all. They were all talking, and then they watched each other hit balls. It was a four-hour clinic of the golf gods…There was a huge gallery of people around. The respect he received was incredible."

On February 20, 1995, the RCGA
finally accepted the nomination of
Moe to the Canadian Golf Hall of
Fame. It was sweet justice for a golfer
whose swing was now respected
around the world as the purest the
game had ever seen. But, it was an
embarrassment to the RCGA which
pretty much had to be guilted into
inducting him. After testimonials
from many world-class golfers
over the course of many years,
how could the RCGA not honour
the brilliance of Moe's swing to
which they had been witness
at such short range for decades?

"I always play 'target golf.'"
—Moe Norman

In 1963, Moe set a world record
by hitting 1,540 balls in just 6 hours
and 51 minutes from an elevated tee
at a driving range in Toronto. More
incredibly, they all went past the
225-yard marker, and they were all
within a 30-yard wide range, an
astonishing measure of consistency.

"Of today's players, I like Vijay Singh the best. I watch him and see how well he gets along with himself. He's not afraid to say what he believes. Of the women, Annika [Sorenstam] is the best, and for the same reason. She's at ease with herself. Watch her when she makes a bogey. She forgets it and goes to the next hole. She knows she's capable of birdieing the next hole." —Moe Norman

Moe's hatred of slow play—and slow for him was anything less than lightning fast—was legendary. "I'm thinking about my next shot while I'm walking up to it," he once said. "Then I hit quick. On the green, I never get down to sight a putt. Never been down in my life. Just walk up and stroke."

Moe ran afoul with the RCGA because of his methods, his clowning, his personality. So, the RCGA revoked Moe's amateur status on the slimmest of technicalities. Moe explained: "I was getting ready to represent Canada in the 1956 America's Cup in Mexico. I had my team jacket, got my inoculations, had my airline tickets. I was excited. I was the Canadian Amateur champion two years running, and I'd be playing against Harvie Ward, the U.S. Amateur champion two years running. Four days before I'm to leave, the Royal Canadian Golf Association convenes a special meeting. From that, I received a letter telling me I wasn't a true amateur, and to please return the jacket and airline tickets. I returned them. I wasn't an amateur by their definition, and I sure wasn't a pro. Where could I play golf?"

Moe bragged that he played more than a decade with the same golf tee. "Hit golf balls, not golf tees," he'd say.

"Negative thinking hurts more than negative swinging."
—Moe Norman

An early story of Moe doing crazy things on the course came from friend John Czarny. He was 17 and Moe 15 when they played a nine-hole course in Walkerton, Ontario. Moe had been golfing seriously for only a year or so. "I put eight Coke bottles down on a tee," Czarny related, "and a ball on each one. There was a tree in the middle of the fairway. Moe asked what kind of shots I wanted—draws, fades, big slices. He hit every shot exactly as I called it." And, not one of those bottles moved an inch.

"One day I met Dave Pelz, the short-game teacher. We were debating, and I told him I could drive the ball straighter than he could putt one. He looked at me funny, and I told him I was serious. "Let's put a post out in the fairway 250 yards away. You choose a hole to putt at from 80 feet away. We'll take turns, and I bet I'll hit the post before you hole a putt." Dave turned down the bet. Dave is going around telling this story, so you know it's true."

—Moe Norman

Moe may not have looked the paradigm of physical health, but he usually filled his golf bag with hundreds of golf balls so that he'd improve his leg strength as he carried his bag around the course. "Got to keep my legs strong," was another of his mantras.

"Hold the club in the palms, not the fingers. How do tennis players hold a tennis racket? In the palm. How do you hold a baseball bat? In the palms. Everyday items—an axe, a hammer—are held in the palms. They're the most sensitive parts of your body. Why would you want to hold a golf club in your fingers? It'll move all over the place!"

—Moe Norman

"If they had a tournament in the dark," Moe said, "I'd be the only one who could play. I'd know where to walk." Straight hitter, straight talker.

"It didn't come to me. I had to work.
I got off this thing," Moe explained,
patting his bum. "The other guys were
playing cards. I was out in the pouring
rain, blood coming down my hands,
that's how much I liked it when I was
a kid, even though it's not a sport like it
is today. It's such a simple thing to hit a
shot. I was like a part of it. I was attached
to my golf shots. I still am. When I hit
a golf ball, I feel like I'm going with it,
like it's pulling me to happiness."

Moe refused to swim because he said
the activity used muscles other than
those needed to golf, and he didn't
want to do anything that might
compromise his swing.

"My childhood was very difficult. We were poor. Me and my brothers used bobby pins to hold our pants up, and we taped our shoes to hold them together. Our father was very strict. When I got a set of clubs together, he wouldn't let me bring them in the house. I knew if he got his hands on them he'd throw them out, so I kept them under the back porch, through a little hole where he couldn't get at them because he was fat. He was pleased when I started getting my name in the newspaper, but he never saw me hit a golf ball, even in our hometown when I became well known."
—Moe Norman

On his fast play:
"I'm the 747 of golf.
One look and I swing."

At the 1954 America's Cup, Moe was playing against the heavily-favoured American, Bill Campbell, and Mexico's Carlos Belmont. On the 34th hole of the 36-hole match-play event, Moe trailed by two strokes and Campbell stuck a tee shot two feet from the pin on the par three. Moe pulled out an 8-iron, and with cool resolve watched his shot land just behind the hole with backspin. The ball rolled into the cup. One reporter famously wrote that, "the unflappable Campbell was flapped." Moe won the 36th hole to force extra holes and clinched the match on the 37th hole.

"The heavier the clubs the better. The swing weight on all my clubs is E-3, and my driver weighs 16 ounces. To get them that heavy, I put lead tape under the grips and on the clubhead. I don't like light clubs. They feel like matchsticks to me and tend to wave all over the place when you swing them. Speed is important, but so is mass."
—Moe Norman

"To help me relax in the car, I listen to Tony Robbins CDs. I love the self-help stuff. My, what a head Tony Robbins has on his shoulders. He's a huge fan of my "Natural Golf" method. Maybe he'll let me go to one of his seminars."

—Moe Norman

After receiving his monthly stipend from Titleist later in life, Moe visited the company's Canadian head office in Gormley, north of Toronto. He'd hit balls and allow Titleist to monitor his swing and measure the ball's trajectory. Incredibly, Moe's shots had no recorded sidespin, only backspin, meaning he hit the ball perfectly dead centre. No other golfer ever hit the ball without sidespin which always accounted for a loss of velocity and, more importantly, accuracy. Said Titleist president Wally Uihlein: "I can verify firsthand that in all of our years of launch-monitor testing, the golf shots of Moe Norman came as close to the perfect impact condition that we ever tested."

The 1955 Canadian Amateur
Championship was played at the
Calgary Golf and Country Club, and
Moe qualified by virtue of being the
runner-up at the Ontario Amateur.
He advanced to the 36-hole match-
play final against Lyle Crawford from
Vancouver, and on the final hole Moe
was 1-up. Crawford birdied, though,
and Moe managed only a par, and
the match continued. Finally, on the
39th hole, Moe birdied for the win,
his first major individual title and
the first time in four years the event
was actually won by a Canadian.
His life was no longer anonymous.

> # "Never let the ball control you—you control the ball."
> # —Moe Norman

One year at the Canadian Amateur Championship, in Calgary, Moe played Gerry McGee in the match-play finals. McGee's slow play so infuriated Moe that Moe took his shoes off and waded in the Bow River looking for golf balls while McGee played.

Bob Tway, winner of many tournaments worldwide including the 1986 PGA Championship and 2003 Canadian Open, was another Moe admirer: "I watched him many, many times. Obviously, [Moe's swing] was a unique style, but if you watched the flight of the ball, it was awfully pure."

Once, at a Canadian amateur tournament, Moe was getting impatient with the slow play of his foursome. When one member bent over to mark his ball on the green, Moe putted between the player's legs, rimming the cup from 40 feet. "All I could see as a target," Moe later said, "was that big rear end."

"My given name is Murray. When I started out as a caddie, a guy started calling me Moe. Actually, he called me "Moe the Schmoe, the Pinochle Pro." It made no sense, but it stuck."
—Moe Norman

Moe appeared on a CBC television program called *Showtime* to demonstrate his swing. Producers set up a cloth canvas and assured Moe of its safety. "You could hit a cannon against it, and the ball wouldn't go through," they said. Moe took out a ball, drove it clean through the canvas, and watched as everyone in studio ducked and dove out of the way of the careening ball.

Moe won the 1956 Canadian Amateur Championship in spectacular fashion. Played at the Edmundston Golf Club in New Brunswick, it was a long test of difficult golf. The semi-final match was the highlight for Moe as he crushed John Miles 8 and 7 in just 29 holes. Moe shot a 64 in the morning, a course record that was so impressive it has yet to be equaled. "That was probably the best round I ever shot in my life," Moe said.

After Rockway Golf Club, a public course where Norman first learned to hit a golf ball, Moe began his life in golf in earnest at the Westmount Golf & Country Club in Kitchener, Ontario. Designed by the great Stanley Thompson, it was run by golf pro Normie Himes, who had played nine seasons in the NHL with the defunct New York Americans (1926-35). Himes, a native of Galt, Ontario, wasn't big, but he could skate and was a respected player before retiring to a life on the links, as it were. He hired Moe as a caddy when the boy was only 12 years old. Himes realized how much Moe loved golf, and he allowed Moe to buy his first clubs through the pro shop for just $1.50, paid in ten-cent increments deducted from his caddying wages. Green fees for 18 holes at Westmount was seventy-five cents.

"To devalue the importance of competition, I count my money. It's not a bad idea to do it before you get out of your car to play golf. Make sure you have plenty in your pocket—I've carried $6,000 in cash just for this purpose—take it out and count all the bills. A round of golf isn't important when I've got $6,000 in my pocket? Hah!"
—Moe Norman

—>≫≪<—

"I hit so many balls I tend to build up a huge callous on the meaty part of my left hand. It gets so thick that from time to time I take a pair of scissors and cut it off. The edge of the callous gets very sharp—if I dragged it across your face I'd draw blood."
—Moe Norman

True story. Moe was a natural left-handed golfer, but lefty clubs were so difficult to find that he taught himself to hit from the right side.

Moe won his first tournament in 1948 when he was 19. It was the Ontario Junior Better-Ball Tournament with partner Gerry Kesselring at the Summit Golf Club in Richmond Hill, Ontario.

PGA Tour veteran Vijay Singh was asked who was the best golfer he'd ever seen. His answer came without pause: "Moe Norman. I've hit balls with him lots of times. He was incredible. Whatever he said he could do, he could do. If you talk to Lee Trevino and the other greats of the game, they'll tell you how good he was. He could talk it, and he could do it. God gives people little gifts, and Moe had a gift for golf."

Rock star Neil Young once played a round of golf on an exotic island with a French golfer who didn't speak English. On one drive, Young hit the ball straight up, and then deadpanned, "Only Moe Norman could do that." His French companion asked, "You know Moe Norman?"

Soon after turning 20, Moe won his first individual golf tournament (a year earlier he had won a tournament partnered with friend Gerry Kesselring). He had to hitchhike to get to the St. Thomas Golf & Country Club Invitational, but despite never having seen the course previously he shot a 67 and won. Ever shy, he didn't wait around to collect his first prize, hitchhiking back home immediately after the victory.

Moe's first pro tournament on the PGA Tour came in January 1959 at the Los Angeles Open, playing against legends including Ben Hogan, Sam Snead, Arnold Palmer, Ken Venturi, and Jimmy Demaret. "For the first time in my life," Moe said, "I knew I was up against the best."

"If you want to be any good at this game, you have to hit 600 balls every day."
—Moe Norman

"I'm good with numbers.
Number of courses played: 434. Number of courses I can remember the exact hole yardages: 375. Age when I saw my first doctor: 68. Number of two-stroke penalties in one 11-year period: only one—I hit a drive that went out-of-bounds by two feet. Most balls hit in one day: 2,207. Total balls hit in my lifetime: About five million, not counting chips and putts."
—Moe Norman

Moe played the Los Angeles Open in January 1959 as a pro. On one hole he sent his approach shot into the bunker causing some fans to sigh with sympathy. "Don't worry," he reassured them, "it's the easiest shot in the bag. In fact, I was shooting for the trap. I can knock the ball out with one hand." One dubious fan suggested $10 would prove him wrong. Moe took the bet, shot with one hand to within two feet of the pin, and tapped in for par, now $10 the richer.

Moe described golf as, "hitting an object to a defined target area with the least amount of effort and an alert attitude of indifference."

Nick Weslock, Moe's friend for more than half a century, made an observation that almost defies logic: "Moe is the only man I ever knew who would wear out a set of irons by creating a hollow about the size of a quarter in the middle of the blade. That was from hitting the ball in exactly the same place, time after time."

Although Moe's childhood was not one of privilege, he wasn't nearly as impoverished as an adult as most thought. He slept in his car and lived a portable life out of desire, not necessity. Once, Moe asked a friend to borrow two dollars. When the friend asked why, Moe said, "I don't want to break a hundred-dollar bill." Most of Moe's savings was in the form of hundred-dollar bills.

"I just learned to putt a short time ago, and now I putt so well it would make you cry. It's the best part of my game, and that's saying a lot."
—Moe Norman

Moe played the 1951 Ontario Amateur,
hosted by the Hunt Club in London.
Ontario Golf Association president
Charlie Watson asked Moe where he was
staying, and Moe informed him he was
sleeping at the nearby football stadium.
Shocked, Watson gave him money for
suitable lodgings, but Moe lost the
money at a poker game later in the day
and continued his residence at the
stadium for the rest of the event.

Said Moe: "All I ever seemed to win
were TV sets. One year I had six,
so I sold them. They [the RCGA]
said I couldn't. I said, 'What am
I supposed to do? Watch all six?'
They said, 'Yes.' So I turned pro."

Hall of Famer Lee Trevino won six
majors and was a contemporary of
Jack Nicklaus, Arnold Palmer, and
Johnny Miller. Trevino was perhaps
the most enthusiastic supporter
of Norman on the PGA Tour:
"I don't know of any player, ever,
who could strike a golf ball like
Moe Norman, as far as hitting
it solid, knowing where it is
going, and knowing what he wants
to do with the ball," Trevino said.

"I've had my fill of competition and
dislike traveling. But my game is
holding up nicely. You know that
show on *The Golf Channel* called
"The Big Break"? I'd win that easily."
—Moe Norman

"Imagination and visualization are keys to my success."
—Moe Norman

Moe liked to walk up to his golf ball from the side rather than from behind, the way all other golfers approached, because this is how he would envision the shot in the end. Why not get used to that view rather than introduce a new one at the critical moment of preparing to hit the ball, he reasoned?

"Crouching down to read a putt is a waste of time. So is plumb-bobbing. You can see all you need standing behind the ball and can feel the slope through your feet when you stand over the ball."
—Moe Norman

Moe's preparation for fairway shots was so brief it appeared as though he walked up to his ball, hit it, and continued to walk up to the green without breaking stride. Once a fan asked Moe if he ever stopped to look at the green before shooting. Said Moe: "Why? Has it moved?"

In a 1988 interview for the television show *The Fifth Estate*, Lee Trevino waxed poetic about Moe's abilities. "Moe is a very shy person, and he doesn't like to be around a lot of people," Trevino explained. "I think if Moe had wanted to be in that situation [the public eye] there is no telling what Moe Norman would have won. I think he would have won the U.S. Open. I think he would have won all the tournaments around the world. I mean, he is that good, and he is still that good."

Moe Norman passed away in 2004 just days before the start of the 100th Canadian Open, played at the Glen Abbey Golf Club just outside Toronto. Most of the caddies wore black pins which featured Moe's name, and flags hung at half-mast. The tournament itself went to extra holes, Vijay Singh beating Canadian Mike Weir on the third hole of sudden death. Singh, a devoted fan of Norman, dedicated the win to the golfer with the perfect swing.

Career Highlights

Canadian Golf Hall of Fame inductee 1995
Played PGA Tour events, 1953-71
Played Senior PGA Tour events, 1981-84

1954 Member of Canada's National Team, America's Cup
1955 & 1956 Canadian Amateur Champion
1956 & 1957 Masters participant
1958 & 1963 Ontario Open Champion
1959 4th at Greater New Orleans Open (best PGA Tour result)
1963 & 1968 Saskatchewan Open Champion
1964 CPGA Miller Trophy Champion
1965-67 Manitoba Open Champion
1966, 1974, 1980 Canadian Professional Golfers Champion
1966, 1971, 1976 Alberta Open Champion
1966 Quebec Open Champion
1971 World Cup National Team
1980-85 & 1987 Canadian Senior Open Champion

Shot 59 three times (last time at age 62)

33 course records

17 holes in one

Acknowledgements

The author would like to thank several people for helping put this book together. To Jason Cheong for help with researching the stories. To the authors whose previous books on Moe provided some of the stories and insight into his legend—Tim O'Connor ("The Feeling of Greatness"), Stan Sauerwein ("Moe Norman"), and the threesome of Lawson Mitchell, Greg Lavern, and Patrick Cunningham ("The Real Moe Norman"). To Todd Graves at www.moenorman.org for photos, encouragement, and support for a man who was important to his own golfing life. To designer Kathryn Zante for breathing new life into Moe's story through unique presentation of these anecdotes. To Kelley Schell and Dave Roy in Kitchener for photos from the Moe Norman Museum at Rockway. To Ed Wilkinson and Dominic Stones for support and collaboration. And to my wife Jane who can hit a pitching wedge pretty well as straight as Moe (not counting a little bend).

Photo Credits

Todd Graves/Graves Golf Academy:
p. 14 (both), photo insert p. 1 (top), 2 (all), 4 (both), 7

John Hamarik/Todd Graves:
photo insert p. 5

Dave Roy/Rockway Golf Club:
p. 9, photo insert p. 1 (bottom), 3, 6 (both), 8